Deserts

By Madeline Boskey

Scott Foresman
is an imprint of

PEARSON

Glenview, Illinois • Boston, Massachusetts • Chandler, Arizona •
Upper Saddle River, New Jersey

Photographs

Every effort has been made to secure permission and provide appropriate credit for photographic material. The publisher deeply regrets any omission and pledges to correct errors called to its attention in subsequent editions.

Unless otherwise acknowledged, all photographs are the property of Pearson Education, Inc.

Photo locators denoted as follows: Top (T), Center (C), Bottom (B), Left (L), Right (R), Background (Bkgd)

Opener George H.H. Huey/Corbis; **1** Bob Krist/Corbis; **3** Jon Bower Dubai 2/Alamy Images; **4** Bob Krist/Corbis; **5** Russ Bishop/Alamy Images; **6** George H.H. Huey/Corbis; **7** (B) Jupiter Images, (T) Rick & Nora Bowers/Alamy Images.

ISBN 13: 978-0-328-50810-5
ISBN 10:   0-328-50810-1

5 6 7 8 9 10 V010 15 14 13 12

Deserts are dry places.
They get very little water.

Deserts are hot early in the day.
They get cool at night.

Deserts are often sandy places.
They can be full of stones.
Winds break the stones into sand.

Deserts are a home for plants.
The plants get water from rain.
They store water in their leaves
and stems.

Deserts are a home for animals.
They go hunting when it gets cool or
at night.
Their eyes often can see in the dark.

Deserts are places people visit.
Would you like visiting a desert?

Think and Share

1. Make a chart like the one below. What was the main idea of this book? Write it in the big oval. Then write some details that tell more about the main idea in the other ovals.

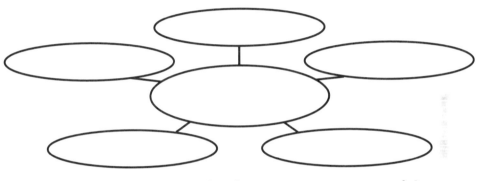

2. What is this book about? Name two things you learned from this book.

3. What is a word that means the opposite of *cool*? Use both words in a sentence.

4. What would be the most interesting thing about visiting a desert? Why?

Science

Genre	Comprehension Skills and Strategy
Expository nonfiction	• Main Idea and Details • Author's Purpose • Important Ideas

Scott Foresman Reading Street 2.1.4

Scott Foresman
is an imprint of

ISBN-13: 978-0-328-50810-5
ISBN-10:   0-328-50810-1

90000 >

9 780328 508105

Making Traveling FUN

by **Michele Spirn**
Illustrated by **Nuri Vergara**

Vocabulary

clearing

crashed

perfect

pond

splashing

spilling

traveled

Word count: 386

Note: The total word count includes words in the running text and headings only. Numerals and words in chapter titles, captions, labels, diagrams, charts, graphs, sidebars, and extra features are not included.